Odysseus and the Cyclops

Tales from the Odyssey

Written by I. M. Richardson
Illustrated by Hal Frenck

Troll Associates

Library of Congress Cataloging in Publication Data

Richardson, I. M.
 Odysseus and the Cyclops.

 (Tales from the Odyssey / adapted by I. M.
Richardson; bk. 2)
 Summary: Odysseus relates to Queen Arete and King
Alcinous his adventures in the land of the Lotus-Eaters
and with the giant Cyclops.
 [1. Mythology, Greek] I. Frenck, Hal, ill.
II. Homer. Odyssey. III. Title. IV. Series:
Richardson, I. M. Tales from the Odyssey; bk. 2.
PZ8.1.R396Tal 1984 bk. 2 292'.13s [292'.13] 83-14236
ISBN 0-8167-0007-9 (lib. bdg.)
ISBN 0-8167-0008-7 (pbk.)

Many years had passed since the Greeks had won the
Trojan War. But one great warrior had still not returned
home to Greece. His name was Odysseus, King of Ithaca.

His long voyage home had been interrupted time and time again. Each delay had brought danger and misfortune. His ships and men had been destroyed. He had managed to survive an ocean storm on a wooden raft. Finally, when the raft had been torn apart, Odysseus had been washed ashore on an island.

The king and queen of the island had agreed to give him swift passage to his home in Ithaca. The ship that would carry him home was anchored in the harbor, and tomorrow it would set sail. Tonight was a time for feasting. It was a time for Odysseus to tell of his adventures.

"After the fall of Troy," said Odysseus, "we conquered a nearby island and divided up the spoils. I thought it best to leave at once, but my men wanted to feast and rest before our long voyage home. While we slept, the enemy brought in reinforcements and made plans to win back their island.

"At dawn, they attacked our ships from both sides. We fought all morning, but by midday, they were getting the upper hand. At last, we raised our anchors and sailed out to sea.

"Soon a terrible storm arose. The wind ripped through our sails and splintered our masts. We had to row our boats to shore, where we found shelter. When the weather cleared, we made repairs and again set sail. But soon another storm was upon us, and we were blown far off our homeward course.

"On the tenth day, we sighted land. After anchoring our ships in a quiet harbor, we went ashore to take on fresh water. After this was done, I sent three men to find out where we were. I did not know it, but we had come to the land of the Lotus-Eaters.

"My men discovered that nothing ever troubled the Lotus-Eaters. They ate the fruit of the lotus to erase their worries and to take away their cares. Of course, the natives offered some of the lotus to their guests. At once, all thoughts of returning to Ithaca were forgotten. My men would have been happy to spend the rest of their days among the Lotus-Eaters.

"When they did not return, I took a party of men and went after them. We had to carry them back to the ships by force, because the lotus had taken away all their cares. Once they were on board, I had to tie them up to keep them from swimming back to shore. Soon we had set sail and were far out to sea.

"We next sailed into a great fog. It was so thick that we could not even see our own masts. Without warning, we ran ashore on a sandy island. The moon was barely visible through the fog, so all we could do was lower our sails and make camp on the beach.

"At dawn, the sun quickly burned away the fog. We had good luck hunting, and soon we were feasting on roast meat. We saw that we were not far from a lovely and inviting land. What we did not know was that it was the land of the Goggle-Eyes. Each of these giants was a Cyclops, who had only one eye.

"I took some of my men and rowed over to the mainland. When we got there, we went ashore to find out what we could. On a cliff overlooking the sea, we found a huge cave. Great tree trunks had been driven into the ground nearby to make a pen for livestock. We wondered who might live here.

14

"Inside the cave, we found great baskets of cheese and huge pots filled with milk and cream. In the corners of the cave were pens filled with young sheep and goats. After we helped ourselves to the cheeses, we sat down to wait for our unknown host. As it turned out, that was not such a good idea.

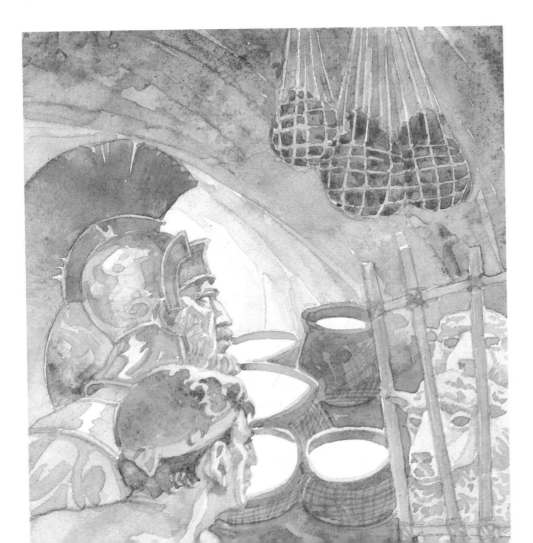

"At last, the Cyclops entered the cave, driving a flock of sheep and goats in front of him. He was so huge and monstrous that we hid ourselves. He threw down a load of firewood and rolled an enormous boulder across the entrance of the cave. Then he lit a blazing fire and milked his sheep and goats.

16

"When he finally saw us, his bellowing filled the cave. I greeted him and told him that we were on our way home from the Trojan War, where we had fought with honor. But instead of greeting us, he reached down and seized two of my men. He lifted them up, kicking and struggling, and then he ate them!

"After he had washed down this meal with warm goat's milk, he lay down among his animals and went to sleep. I thought about driving my sword between his ribs as he slept, but I decided against it. If the Cyclops were not alive to roll the boulder away from the entrance, how would we get out of the cave? For now, all we could do was wait.

"In the morning, old Goggle-Eye seized two more of my men and ate them for breakfast. Then he took his sheep and goats outside and blocked the door again. I looked around the cave and saw a long wooden pole. The Cyclops had cut it to use as a walking stick, but it was as large as the mast of a ship. As I looked at the pole, I began to form a plan for our escape.

"Before long, I had sharpened the end of the pole and made it smooth. Then my men and I lifted it and set the pointed end into the fire. It was freshly cut wood, so it did not burn. This was just as I had hoped. Next, we carried this enormous weapon to the side of the cave and hid it.

"That evening, after the Cyclops had eaten, I offered him a taste of some very strong wine I had brought with me. He took it and drank it in one gulp. 'Give me more,' he roared, 'and tell me your name!' Then I replied, 'My name is Noman.' When he had finished all the wine, he fell asleep and began snoring loudly.

"Then we brought out the sharpened pole and buried the point in the fire. When it was glowing, we held it above the monster's head, and plunged it deep into his eye. It hissed as we drove the pole deeper and deeper. The Cyclops awoke, screaming and clutching his eye. We fled to the darkest corners and hid.

22

"His cries brought his friends to the entrance of the cave. 'Why do you cry out so loudly?' they asked. And he answered. 'Because Noman has blinded me!' Then his friends went away, saying, 'If no man has blinded you, then it must be the work of the gods. In that case, you will just have to suffer.'

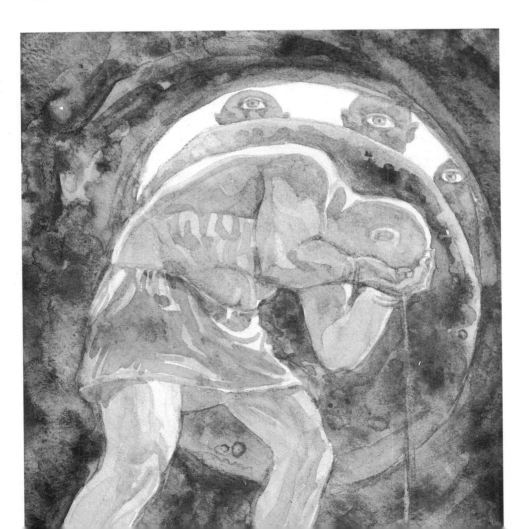

"In the morning, the Cyclops felt around until he found the boulder. He rolled it away and sat down at the entrance of the cave. As his sheep and goats went out past him, he felt along their backs to make sure we did not sneak out with them. But I had tied my men underneath the stomachs of the animals, and he did not discover them.

"I myself held on to the belly of the largest ram. When the Cyclops passed his hands over its back, he recognized it, and said, 'So, Fleecy-Back, it is you. If only you could speak, I know you would tell me where that wicked Noman is hiding. Then I would make him pay for burning out my eye.' Finally, he let the big ram go out to pasture.

"As soon as I was free, I untied my men, and we herded the sheep and goats together. Soon we had loaded them all aboard our ship. As we rowed out into the harbor, I raised my voice and called back, 'Say there, Cyclops! It looks as if little Noman has outwitted you after all!'

'When he heard this, the Cyclops flew into a rage. He roared and tore off a great chunk of rock, which he hurled in the direction of my voice. The rock whistled over our heads, and plunged into the water in front of us. It made a great wave that drove our ship backward until we ran aground.

"We pushed off the shore and rowed for our very lives. When we were farther away than before, I called back, 'I say, Cyclops! If anyone asks who blinded you, be sure to say it was I—Odysseus, King of Ithaca and conqueror of Troy.' Hearing this, old Goggle-Eye roared louder than before.

"He cried out, 'An old soothsayer once said that I would lose my sight at the hands of Odysseus. Now his prophesy has come true. But my father is Poseidon, the god of the ocean, and he will see to it that you are punished. I will ask him to make you suffer, and lose your companions, and find trouble at home after you return to Ithaca.'

"We quickly rowed back to the sandy island where I had left the rest of my ships and men. First, we divided the sheep evenly among the different ships. Then we spent the rest of the day feasting and telling our companions about our adventure. When the sun finally slipped below the horizon, we fell into a sound sleep.

"At dawn, we boarded our ships and set our course for Ithaca. But the threat of the Cyclops had not been an idle one. I was destined to suffer more hardships and misfortunes, to lose my men, to lose my ships, and finally, to be washed ashore on this island."

Odysseus paused after this long story and raised his cup to the king and queen. They had taken him in when he had been washed ashore on their island. They had launched the ship that would take him on the final leg of his journey. And tomorrow, that ship would take him to Ithaca. His odyssey would finally be over. He was going home at last!